I'M IN THE BAND

Finding a music style

Adam Miller

Raintree is an imprint of Capstone Global Library Limited, a company incorporated in England and Wales having its registered office at 7 Pilgrim Street, London, EC4V 6LB – Registered company number: 6695582

www.raintreepublishers.co.uk
myorders@raintreepublishers.co.uk

Text © Capstone Global Library Limited 2015
First published in hardback in 2014
Paperback edition first published in 2015
The moral rights of the proprietor have been asserted.

Edited by Clare Lewis, Mandy Robbins, Penny West and James Benefield
Designed by Steve Mead
Original illustrations © Capstone Global Library Ltd 2015
Picture research by Ruth Blair
Production by Victoria Fitzgerald
Originated by Capstone Global Library Ltd
Printed and bound in China by CTPS

ISBN 978 1 406 28250 4 (hardback)
18 17 16 15 14
10 9 8 7 6 5 4 3 2 1

ISBN 978 1 406 28255 9 (paperback)
19 18 17 16 15
10 9 8 7 6 5 4 3 2 1

British Library Cataloguing in Publication Data
A full catalogue record for this book is available from the British Library.

Acknowledgements
We would like to thank the following for permission to reproduce photographs: Corbis pp. 23 (© EPA/MARTA PEREZ), 24 (© Greg Hinsdale), 25 (© Roger Ressmeyer); Getty Images pp. 7 bottom, 7 top, 8 top, 18 top, 21, 37 (Michael Ochs Archive), 8 bottom (Walter looss Jr./Getty Images), 9, 41 (David Redfern/Redferns), 10, 11, 19 (Ebet Roberts/Redferns), 14 bottom left (Mick Hutson/Redferns), 15 botom left (Christopher Furlong), 15 top left (JOE KLAMAR/AFP), 16 (Phil Dent/Redferns), 17 (Chris Walter/WireImage), 18 bottom, 19 top (Michael Putland), 20 (James Devaney), 22 (© 2011 NBAE/Garrett Ellwood), 28 (Sean Murphy), 29 (Roberta Bayley/Redferns), 30 top (WireImage), 31 (Roberta Bayley/Redferns), 32, 33 (Lex van Rossen/MAI/Redferns), 34 (Jason Kempin/FilmMagic), 35 (BIPS); Shutterstock pp. 5 (Goran Djukanovic), 13 (sandsun), 14 bottom right (arek_malang), 14 top left (Christian Bertrand), 14 top right (Gina Smith), 15 top right (Kiselev Andrey Valerevich), 30 bottom (Mat Hayward); Superstock pp. 26, 27 (Purestock), 36 (Flirt), 40 (Radius).

Artistic Effects: Shutterstock.

Cover photograph reproduced with permission of Getty Images (Peeter Viisimaa).

We would like to thank Matt Anniss for his invaluable help in the preparation of this book.

Contents

YOU GOTTA HAVE STYLE!

Have you ever wanted to put together a band? If so, what would the band be like? Working this out seems quite simple, but a lot goes into it. What kind of music would the band play? How would the band look and present itself?

Of course, the most important part is always writing and performing the songs well, but your band's look, style and attitude are also important. What kind of music do you love to listen to? Do most of your favourite artists have a similar sound? Do they have a similar look? Or do some go outside the mould?

Solo to band

Even solo artists need to think about how their style of music will come across when they perform on stage. Artists like Madonna or Beyoncé put a lot of thought into how their live band will look and perform. They think about whether they will be supported by dancers, special effects or maybe both. All of this is part of the style they project when they are performing live.

PLAYING LIVE IN FRONT OF AN AUDIENCE CAN BE AN AMAZING EXPERIENCE!

BANDSPEAK

A genre is simply another way of saying musical style. Punk, hip-hop, electronic and country are all genres. There are sub-genres, too. For instance, Skrillex is an electronic artist, but he performs a specific style known as dubstep. Taylor Swift is usually known as a country artist, but the genre she performs is country pop. There are even sub-genres of sub-genres!

HOW DIFFERENT MUSIC STYLES DEVELOP

There are so many different types of music in the world. Each genre and sub-genre has its own look and musical style associated with it.

Different strokes for different folks

Most genres develop from earlier genres. For example, early rock and roll musicians, such as Chuck Berry, Little Richard and Elvis Presley, seemed new and wild in the mid-1950s. But the rhythms of new rock and roll weren't that different to the earlier music of big band leaders like Louis Jordan and Fats Waller. Instead of a big band, rock and roll just used a few instruments, such as drums, bass, guitar, piano and sometimes a saxophone. Some country influences could be heard in rock and roll, as well. However, the style of the early rockers, with their slicked-back hair and "bad-boy" look, was new.

In the mid-1960s, a series of bands from England became very successful in the United States. This was known as the "British Invasion". Led by the Beatles, these bands were inspired by early rock and roll acts as well as the rhythm and blues (R&B) coming out of the United States. The rock bands that we see today are at least in some part influenced by these 1960s British bands.

Did you know?

Much of popular music today can be traced back to the musical traditions of African American slaves. For example, the call and response musical tradition of African American slaves can be seen as an ancestor of rapping.

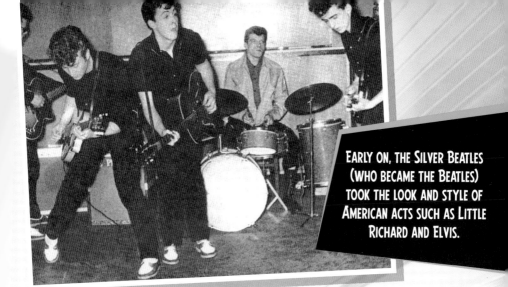

Buddy Holly was a tall, skinny American rock and roll star with thick glasses. His look was very different from the cool, rebellious look of other rockers. But Holly's look has never gone out of fashion. Elvis Costello, David Byrne, Morrissey and Devo have all borrowed the look. Even Lady Gaga has been known to wear Buddy Holly glasses.

Did you Know?

Many famous bands and artists stand out because they have their own unique style. They do not copy others but do their own thing, and become famous for their unique look. Can you come up with a unique style for you and your band?

What influences a style of music?

Besides the roots of a genre, there can be outside factors that influence a particular music style.

JEFFERSON AIRPLANE DISPLAYED THE HIPPIE LOOK OF THE LATE 1960S.

Politics

Over the years, politics has played a huge role in music. During the 1960s, a lot was happening in the world. The Vietnam War (1959–1975) was unpopular, the civil rights movement was taking off in the United States and women were joining the struggle for equal treatment. This had a big influence on the music of the time. Folk songs by artists such as Bob Dylan and Joan Baez seemed to capture the feelings of political unrest. At Martin Luther King Jr's 1963 March on Washington, Baez and Dylan performed to a huge crowd of protesters.

Did you know?

Aretha Franklin's most popular song was "Respect". Recorded in 1967, it seemed to speak to everything going on in the world at the time: the civil rights movement in the United States, women's rights around the world and even the Vietnam War.

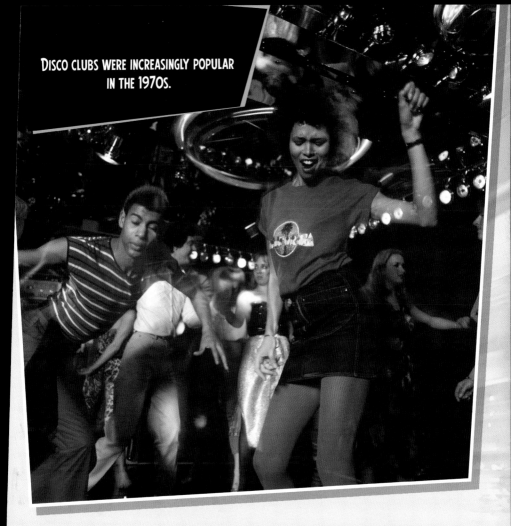

At the very end of the 1960s, many young people became disillusioned with trying to change the world. The Vietnam War was still raging on. By the end of the decade, Martin Luther King, Malcolm X and John F. Kennedy had been killed. Unemployment was high and many people were struggling for money. People were looking for escapism and found it through music. Disco music was all about partying and dancing the night away. The bright colours and patterns that characterized the 1970s also reflected this attitude.

Place

Musical styles can be tied to the countries where people live. For example, ska is a genre that developed in Jamaica during the late 1950s, as radios became popular in the country. These radios were able to tune into stations from relatively nearby cities in the southern United States, such as New Orleans, that were playing jazz and R&B. These styles then became popular in Jamaica. Ska is an upbeat style that takes these American influences and blends them with Caribbean music. At the time, Jamaica was still part of the British Commonwealth. So, during the early 1960s ska music travelled to the United Kingdom.

Living conditions

Similarly, neighbourhoods where people live can influence music. The roots of hip-hop are in funk, disco, soul, reggae and even in slavery (see the box on page 6). However, many hip-hop lyrics have been about the poor and dangerous neighbourhoods where rappers lived. One of the most popular early rap hits was Grandmaster Flash and The Furious Five's "The Message" released in 1982. The storyteller describes the conditions he is living under in the South Bronx of New York City. The lyrics brought mainstream attention to the crime, drug abuse and poor schools that often characterized life in neglected neighbourhoods.

BandSpeak

MC is short for master of ceremonies. You could say the MC is the microphone controller!

"The Message" was a total knock out of the park. Grandmaster Flash and the Furious Five was the first dominant rap group with the most dominant MC saying something that meant something.

Chuck D of Public Enemy

GRANDMASTER FLASH AND THE FURIOUS FIVE WAS ONE OF THE FIRST WELL-KNOWN HIP-HOP GROUPS.

How has hip-hop changed over the years?

Once styles of music have developed, they change over time. Some styles can peak and eventually fade away. Others, like hip-hop, continue to evolve.

The birth of hip-hop music can be traced back to the Bronx in New York City in the 1970s. Dance parties were often held where DJs would extend certain sections of songs that dancers enjoyed. DJs would also talk over these sections. The talking led to rappers, known as MCs, speaking simple rhymes over the beats to hype up the dance floor. This eventually became what is now known as rap music or hip-hop.

BANDSPEAK

Breakbeats – Most R&B, funk and pop songs have a small instrumental sequence in them. DJs call these the breakbeats. Using two copies of a record on two turntables, early hip-hop DJs isolated the breakbeats and extended them to keep the party going! Later, these breaks were sampled (recorded and looped) and used as backing tracks for hip-hop music.

Soon, drum machines were added to create more forceful beats and rappers developed their own styles and got increasingly better. As technology allowed DJs and producers to come up with more complex beats, rappers developed more unique and complicated rhymes. Both sides have worked together to forge new sounds and styles. Rap music has become much more sophisticated since its early days.

Big business

Today, professional hip-hop producers create beats and sell them to rappers for large sums of money. Likewise, some up-and-coming artists will pay a lot of money to have a well-known rapper contribute a rap on a track.

DJs STILL PLAY VINYL RECORDS IN CLUBS.

Which came first: the fashion Or the music ?

FOLK FASHION: IS NOT CARING ABOUT A STYLE, A STYLE IN ITSELF?

THIS HAIRCUT LETS YOU KNOW THIS PERSON IS A PUNK!

THIS "ROCK" STYLE WAS POPULAR IN THE 1980S.

SOME PEOPLE GO FOR THE COUNTRY LOOK...

Fashion and music go together. Sometimes it is impossible to work out which came first. They can seem to have developed together. Over the years, various music styles have taken on some very memorable looks! Let's take hairstyles as an example.

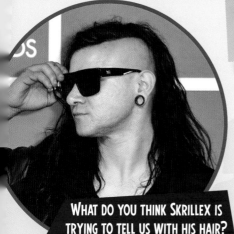

WHAT DO YOU THINK SKRILLEX IS TRYING TO TELL US WITH HIS HAIR?

GOTHS WANT YOU TO KNOW THEY ARE EDGY.

THIS 1950S HAIRSTYLE SUGGESTS ROCK AND ROLL!

Style icons

Some musicians seem to create their own styles from out of the blue. Let's take the 1980s as an example. The singer Michael Jackson will always be remembered for his single white glove, sequinned jackets and sparkly white socks, and introducing the moonwalk to a television audience. Prince, with his outrageous purple outfits, stylized facial hair and athletic dance moves gave fans of his funk something to pay attention to. In the 1980s, Madonna, with her gummy bracelets, vintage clothes and messy hair gave birth to an army of "Madonna wannabes" who copied her look.

Michael Jackson had been a famous **Did you know?** performer since he was a very young child. But, in 1983, when he released his album *Thriller*, his level of fame exploded. Suddenly, everyone wanted to wear a red leather motorcycle jacket like the one Michael Jackson wore in the "Beat It" video!

MICHAEL JACKSON WAS ONE OF THE STYLE ICONS OF THE 1980S.

The rock star look

Keith Richards, guitarist in the British rock band The Rolling Stones, was key in developing what we know as the rock star look. This look usually consists of messy hair, sunglasses, skinny jeans, tight T-shirts, vintage scarves, bandanas and big silver rings. Rock stars with this look have a dishevelled style that suggests they just threw on whatever was on the floor! Nearly every rock star that came after Keith Richards has borrowed his look in at least a small way.

JUST ONE LOOK AT KEITH RICHARDS' HAIR TELLS YOU THAT HE IS A ROCK STAR.

Keith Richards' wild look might have helped him win the role of a pirate in two of the *Pirates of the Caribbean* movies, starring Johnny Depp!

Did you know?

INSPIRED

David Bowie

David Bowie started his musical career in London in the mid-1960s and has gone through many stylistic and visual changes. He shows that your style can change over the years but should always be personal to you, and be about both your music and your look.

Lift off

Bowie's first big hit, "Space Oddity", was released in the summer of 1969, just five days before the Apollo 11 launch that sent astronauts to the Moon. The song was about an astronaut stranded in his spacecraft. At this time, Bowie's image was that of a freaky, space-age folk rocker. He had spiky hair, red boots and shimmering clothes of odd colours, patterns and fabrics.

DAVID, THE FRESH-FACED FOLK SINGER.

ZIGGY STARDUST: SHINY AND THEATRICAL.

The rise and fall of Ziggy Stardust

In 1972, Bowie reinvented himself as Ziggy Stardust, a wild, flame-haired alien who loved bizarre outfits and loud guitars. Concerts during the Ziggy years involved many costume changes, theatrical lighting, and lots of make-up! Though other bands were performing this kind of glam rock, Bowie really introduced the world to the style.

The Thin White Duke

Bowie's music slowly became less glam and more soulful. As the music changed, so did his look. In 1976, he was fully into a new character, the elegant, icy and distant Thin White Duke. The music during these years was heavily influenced by electronic music coming out of Germany by bands such as Kraftwerk.

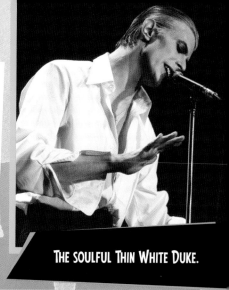

THE SOULFUL THIN WHITE DUKE.

The pop icon

In the 1980s, Bowie became a blonde, well-dressed pop star. In 1983, he released *Let's Dance*, a pure pop album with a series of hit singles. Videos of the songs were played on a new channel, MTV. Bowie was now a pop icon!

IN THE 1980S, DAVID BOWIE WAS A POP MEGASTAR.

David Bowie has also acted in movies and has experimented in many other genres of music. In 2013, he released another critically acclaimed album, *The Next Day*.

In 2013, the Victoria and Albert Museum in London ran an exhibition that looked at Bowie's influential career.

Did you know?

19

Can a band be a brand?

While some bands only play music for the love of it, or to get a political message out, most bands dream of making it big one day. To do that, you will need talent and luck. You will also need to think about music as a business.

I'm not a businessman, I'm a business, man!

Jay Z

When Jay Z (sometimes known as Jay-Z) describes himself as a business (see quotation above), he doesn't mean he gets up every morning to work in a office. He means he is the brand itself. As well as being a very talented and successful rapper, Jay Z has worked with many different businesses. In 2013, he famously made a deal with Samsung Mobile.

Buyers of their new phone would be able to download Jay Z's new album several days before it was released to the buying public.

JAY Z HAS A VERY FAMOUS WIFE: BEYONCE!

BandSpeak

Many bands have a gimmick, something different that makes them stand out. An early example of this is The Who. They were known for smashing their instruments after some of their performances. Other examples involve make-up and costumes. The Flaming Lips are known for putting on fun, festival-like performances with glitter, dancers dressed as animals and frontman Wayne Coyne rolling out into the crowd inside a giant plastic bubble!

The rock band KISS, known for dressing as comic-book-style superheroes, alienated a lot of their fan base when they decided to stop wearing make-up. Eventually, the costumes and make-up went back on and their career was revived!

Did you Know?

Substance over style

While the outrageous style and glamorous shows of some performers can certainly be entertaining, it can also be refreshing to see someone like Kelly Clarkson or lesser known singer-songwriters like Ted Leo, who dress very naturally. Different styles, looks and approaches work for different acts. The important thing is to find what works for you and what you're comfortable with.

KELLY CLARKSON DOESN'T RELY ON FANCY COSTUMES.

BAND TECH

If you want to get serious, a logo is a great marketing tool. A logo is the same as a brand label. It is a designed piece of artwork that can be used on flyers, posters, stickers, T-shirts, pin badges, on a stage backdrop and maybe even the bass drum. Many bands you like probably have their name in a certain typeface and style that does not change. The Rolling Stones' mouth and tongue logo is a good example. Designing a good logo can be hard. You need a logo that is original and cool but simple enough to remember.

Walk the line

Of course, many artists achieve both skilled, thoughtful music and outrageous style. Lady Gaga is known for her unique outfits and performances. But she writes her own songs and her music is admired by fans and critics alike. The German electronic band, Kraftwerk, have always portrayed a robotic image. In live shows, they are known for bringing out robotic versions of each member who take over the show for a few songs. But their melodic tunes introduced the world to electronic music and influenced countless other acts.

I think fashion and music go hand in hand, and they always should. It is the artist's job to create imagery that matches the music...

Lady Gaga

KRAFTWERK: MEN OR MACHINES?

BANDSPEAK

A fan base is a band's core group of fans. The fan base is the people who try to see every show, buy all of the music and tell other people about the band. A fan base ranges in size from a few dozen to several million people, but every act, large or small, needs to build a fan base.

Finding your own style

Have you and your band settled on a style of music yet? If not, you will need to work that out soon. It should be pretty easy — what kind of music do you and your band like to listen to? If your tastes differ, is there at least some crossover?

FINDING YOUR STYLE AND SOUND CAN BE HARD ... BUT IT'S WORTH IT!

Coming up with your own sound

What if you like loud and fast rock and roll music, but the drummer is into hip-hop, the bass player listens to jazz and your singer loves electronic dance music? How are you going to make your music work so that everyone is happy? It might not be easy, but try to find some overlap. This will not only make you all get along better but, if you are good enough, you just might create a new sound! Not many bands can say they developed a new genre. Embrace your differences and make it work.

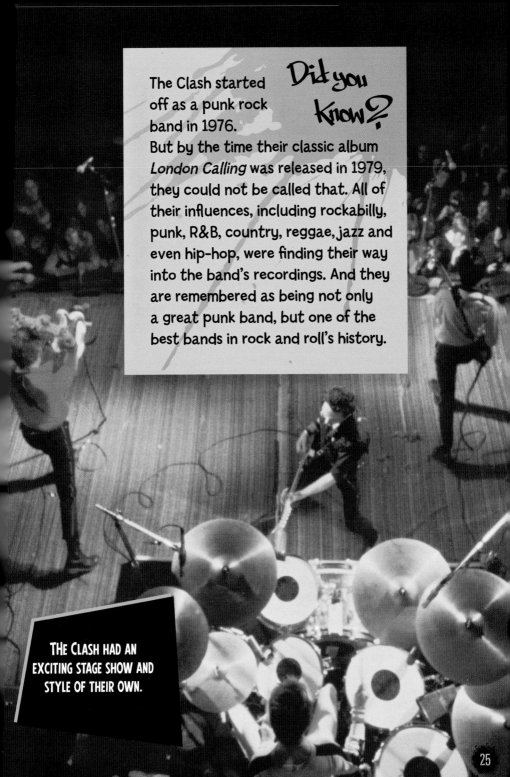

Did you Know?

The Clash started off as a punk rock band in 1976. But by the time their classic album *London Calling* was released in 1979, they could not be called that. All of their influences, including rockabilly, punk, R&B, country, reggae, jazz and even hip-hop, were finding their way into the band's recordings. And they are remembered as being not only a great punk band, but one of the best bands in rock and roll's history.

THE CLASH HAD AN EXCITING STAGE SHOW AND STYLE OF THEIR OWN.

Being original!

Of course, it is possible that all your bandmates have similar influences. You have started a band together after all! Start by playing some of everyone's favourite songs. Keep playing them and learn how your heroes do it.

But you don't want to turn into a karaoke version of a successful band, so you will need your own songs. Coming up with a tune is hard work, but practice will get you there. Maybe the drummer has a good beat he has been playing. Get him to start and then the others can jump in when they are ready. Or if the guitarist has a riff, maybe that is where the rest will fall into place. Some songwriters start with the words. If you have some lyrics, see if you can put them to a melody by humming them.

BAND TECH

Do you know what it means to jam? Jamming can start with a drumbeat, a bass line, or a guitar or keyboard riff. Others can jump in when they start to feel the groove, adding more layers. After a while, the music you are making might take some unexpected turns. It is these turns that might help you to work out your own sound or style.

THE BEST WAY TO FIND A STYLE IS TO LET IT COME OUT OF YOUR MUSIC.

BandSpeak

Plagiarism is copying another artist's work. It is very natural to be influenced by other people's music and it is usually okay to cover songs by your favourite artists if you are playing live and for free. But you can't record or make any money from other people's music unless you have clear permission from the writer of the song.

You got the look!

Your look will depend on the type of band you want to be. Some acts are very casual, looking like they just woke up and put on whatever they could find. Others have amazing costumes and make-up that took hours to put on. One thing is certain – both types put some thought into how they want to present themselves.

Looking good without spending a fortune

You don't need a lot of money to find cool outfits. In fact, it can be fun scouring second-hand shops with friends, hunting for perfect clothes. Maybe you have got some old clothes that don't fit any more. Is there anything you can do with the fabric? Vintage is always in fashion. Maybe there is some old fabric lying around your home that no one is using, which could be used to make an outfit. Or can it be sewn onto something else? Imagination is much more important than cash when it comes to finding the right look!

IN SEARCH OF A PERFECT LOOK?
TRY VISITING A CHARITY SHOP.

28

The invention of a new look

Richard Hell, lead singer in an early punk band from New York called the Voidoids, is said to have created the punk look. He often wrote slogans on his T-shirts and cut his clothes into pieces. Then he would pin them back together with safety pins. Malcolm McLaren, a fashion designer and band manager from London, saw Richard Hell's unique look and kept it in mind when he went back to the United Kingdom. He started selling similar slogan T-shirts and pinned-together clothing in his shop. He also put together the Sex Pistols, the most famous punk band of the time, and made sure they all dressed in a punk rock style.

RICHARD HELL, ROCKING THE PUNK LOOK IN 1977.

THE TOTAL PACKAGE!

When you have some cool songs and a great look, it is time to think about how you will appear on stage. Whether you have carefully choreographed moves or your style is more laid-back, you need to look comfortable on stage. Film yourselves practising. How do you look? The more you practise and watch yourself perform, the more confident you will feel when playing live.

DEVO PLAY ROBOTICALLY AND WEAR QUIRKY COSTUMES.

MUMFORD AND SONS LOOK CASUAL AND A LITTLE OLD-FASHIONED.

THE RAMONES ALWAYS PERFORMED IN JEANS, T-SHIRTS AND LEATHER JACKETS.

The stage show

You can just step on stage with your instruments and play. However, some bands put a little more into their show.

Backdrop

A backdrop featuring the name of your band or your band's logo is a great thing to pin up. These can be professionally printed, but can also be made on an old sheet or a piece of board.

Lighting

Some concerts have amazing lightshows with massive floodlights, lasers, spinning contraptions and projected images or film. This can quickly get expensive, but it doesn't need to. A simple mirror ball can be hung above the stage with a light pointing at it, creating the effect of stars spinning around the band and audience. Likewise, think about using coloured filters over the lights. You can even set up a blank sheet to act as a screen. If you can borrow a projector, a friend could put images, show film or even mix oil and coloured water to create cool effects on stage!

BAND TECH

Guitar straps are there to hold up your guitar, but they can also make a statement about the type of band you are. Bands like Nirvana and the Ramones had their guitars hanging low for a rock and roll look, while the Beatles wore them high up. Of course, you could just keep them wherever they feel most comfortable!

INSPIRED

The White Stripes

The White Stripes consisted of only two people, Jack and Meg White. But with great songs, unique style and nearly constant touring, they quickly went from a little-known band from Detroit in the United States to international stardom.

Do it yourself

The White Stripes started in 1997. Jack played the guitar and sang, while Meg thumped away on the drums, creating a stripped down but heavy sound. Their music breathed new life into blues-based rock, but their image was also memorable. They used a bold red and white colour scheme, creating a simple yet striking look. Before they became successful they did this on a small scale, wearing red or white T-shirts and red or white jeans, playing red and white instruments, and using red and white lighting and backdrops. They arranged their own tours, travelling around with their gear in a small car.

Becoming Famous

Around 2001, The White Stripes were becoming well known internationally. They took the red and white theme to the next level, with custom-made red and white suits and stage sets. After a very successful decade, the White Stripes called it quits in 2011.

While The White Stripes' music was critically acclaimed, the sharp image and blistering concerts all played into their massive success. Today, Jack White still performs as a solo artist and with other bands.

THE WHITE STRIPES' DISTINCTIVE LOOK HELPED THEM GET NOTICED.

Did you Know?

When The White Stripes first became famous, people wondered about their relationship. Jack and Meg claimed they were brother and sister but rumours still spread. Eventually, it was discovered that they had been married at one point. Jack took Meg's surname, White, and they remained close friends. The intrigue surrounding their relationship certainly didn't hurt the band's popularity!

Who are you?

Maybe you don't have any desire to put your face out in front of the crowds. That is okay! And never showing yourself can even create a buzz. Several musicians and bands release music without ever revealing themselves. The popular British band Gorillaz was unique, not only because their sound combined lots of different genres, but because each member was represented by a cartoon character. In fact, a key member of the band was comic-book artist Jamie Hewlett. He didn't play an instrument but he created the backstory for the characters and all of the imagery. Live shows consisted of the band playing behind a screen. The screen showed the animated Gorillaz playing the songs. It was an interesting and very successful concept.

GORILLAZ: REAL, LIVE COMIC
BOOK CHARACTERS?

THE BEATLES' POPULARITY GREW EVEN WHEN THEY STOPPED PLAYING LIVE!

The Beatles stopped playing live in 1966 but it certainly didn't hurt their success. They were very famous by this time and had grown tired of audiences screaming so loudly that no one could hear them. Not playing live also gave them an air of mystery. The Beatles ended up releasing their most memorable and respected albums after they stopped playing live.

A band mght work anonymously for their entire career, without anyone knowing who they really are. The Residents have been releasing albums for many years. When they perform, they wear creepy masks, such as giant eyeballs wearing top hats. For decades, people have tried to work out who the band is, or if they are a revolving line-up of members. Nobody knows for sure!

Growing and changing

As your musical style develops, and you get better at playing together and feel more comfortable performing, you might find that your sound begins to change. Don't fight it! You have to allow yourself freedom to grow as artists. A band that starts off with loud guitar rock might take on electronic or even jazzy elements later on that transform it into something completely new. The British band Radiohead are a good example of this. They started as a rock band, but have absorbed many musical influences over the years and now have an electronic sound. You might find your own music style goes down a road you didn't expect. Go with it and see where other influences might lead you.

BE TRUE TO YOURSELF AND YOUR MUSIC.

Old look or new look?

Whether the style of music you play changes or not over time, you should never feel that you have to stick to a certain look. If you started to play wearing weird costumes and feel like this style is getting old, try playing in T-shirts, jeans and trainers. Whatever makes you and your band feel good is what matters.

The legendary songwriter and performer Bob Dylan first found fame performing political folk music, with only an acoustic guitar and a harmonica. In 1965, he was becoming bored with the strict rules of the folk scene and decided to go electric. When he first introduced the world to this new sound at the Newport Folk Festival in 1965, much of the audience was shocked. They booed their hero for playing what they believed was commercial rock and roll music. However, some of his most memorable songs and albums were released post-electric, and his fan base kept growing.

Did you Know?

BOB DYLAN DIDN'T MIND OFFENDING HIS FAN BASE TO CHANGE HIS SOUND.

What's the best path?

Use this flowchart to work out the best musical path for you!

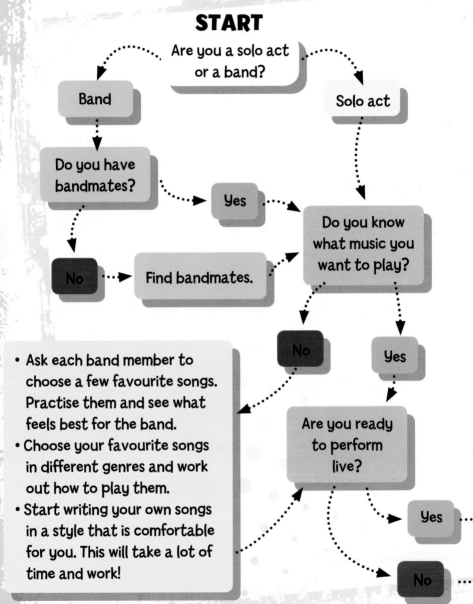

START

Are you a solo act or a band?

Band

Solo act

Do you have bandmates?

Yes

No

Find bandmates.

Do you know what music you want to play?

No

Yes

- Ask each band member to choose a few favourite songs. Practise them and see what feels best for the band.
- Choose your favourite songs in different genres and work out how to play them.
- Start writing your own songs in a style that is comfortable for you. This will take a lot of time and work!

Are you ready to perform live?

Yes

No

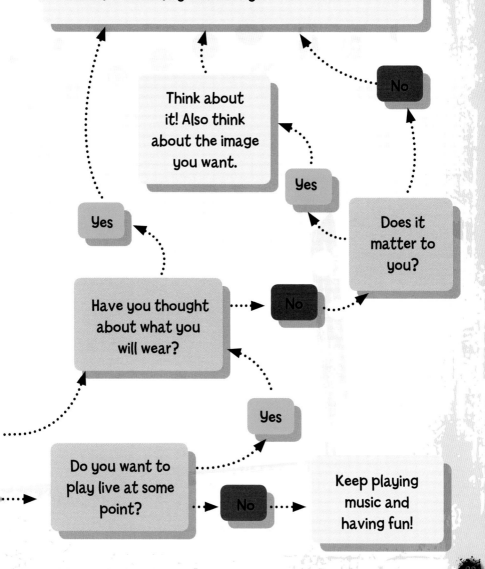

You have worked out what your genre is and have your own style! Keep on practising and listening to music you haven't heard before. You will keep getting better and better. Pretty soon, you should consider recording some songs.

No

Think about it! Also think about the image you want.

Yes

Yes

Does it matter to you?

Have you thought about what you will wear?

No

Yes

Do you want to play live at some point?

No

Keep playing music and having fun!

CREATING THE band

Being in a band is a fun and rewarding experience, even if it is just a hobby. Of course, you will become better at playing an instrument and/or singing. But you will also become a better listener and appreciate music more.

Sssh! Listen...

As you listen to more and more music in different genres, you will start to hear the influences of your favourite bands. Listening to many styles of music is a good way to not only work out what you like and don't like, but it can also inspire you and give you some great ideas! Once you work out which genres you like the most, you can dig deep into the artists that influenced your favourite artists. Having a large base of musical knowledge makes it easier to develop your own musical style.

YOUR BAND'S SOUND AND LOOK IS ENTIRELY UP TO YOU AND YOUR BANDMATES.

Feeling good is what's important

Some bands love dressing up and looking the part. Others don't seem to care and wear a mixture of different outfits. At the end of the day, the only thing that matters is that you and the other members feel like you are all a part of something. As you play together and develop a musical style, you might find you start developing a group fashion sense, as well!

JIMI HENDRIX IS STILL A STYLE AND MUSICAL INFLUENCE TODAY.

Jimi Hendrix died in 1970, but he is still considered to be one of the most influential guitarists who ever lived. And his fashion sense was pretty memorable, too!

Did you Know?

QUIZ

Finding a music style isn't always obvious or easy. Try this multiple-choice quiz to help you to decide what to do next.

1 Compared to your friends, how would you rate your musical knowledge?
- **a)** I listen to a lot of music, but I wouldn't call myself a music expert.
- b) If I am honest, I know very little but I have heard stuff I enjoy.
- c) I know a lot about music, from the stuff my parents grew up with, to today's latest sounds. Jazz, funk, punk, soul, hip-hop, you name it!

2 For Halloween, I like to...
- **a)** Spend weeks creating the most outrageous costume I can come up with.
- **B)** Put on a mask and go out with friends.
- **c)** Give out sweets. I really don't like wearing costumes.

3 Do you like being out in front of people?
- **a)** Yes! I crave attention. And if I say so myself, I am the life of the party!
- b) I don't mind it, but it's not why I got into playing in a band.
- c) I see it as a necessary evil.

4 I am happiest when:
- **a)** I am the centre of attention.
- b) Our band is practising.
- c) I am listening to great music I have never heard before.

5 How fashionable are you?
  a) Extremely!
  b) It's not something I take too seriously, but I think I look okay.
  c) Fashion, for me, is whatever I have decided to throw on that morning.

6 In art class...
  a) I always get good marks. I love drawing and designing.
  b) I'm okay, I suppose.
  c) I can't even draw a stick figure.

7 How creative do you think you are?
  a) I don't like to boast, but I am extremely creative!
  b) I haven't really thought about it.
  c) Well, I like writing songs and playing music. That's quite creative, isn't it?

Answers

IF YOU ANSWERED MOSTLY AS: Wow. Your band is going to be a lot of fun to see live! At this rate, you could be your generation's David Bowie or Jack White! Keep pushing yourself to try something new, both in terms of your music and your look.

IF YOU ANSWERED MOSTLY BS: Sounds like you are just in it for fun right now. That's great! Keep practising with your bandmates. Keep exposing your ears to more music. Experiment with your sound by jamming. The style will come naturally. For now, just keep on playing and have fun.

IF YOU ANSWERED MOSTLY CS: Music is clearly in your blood. You should have no problem choosing a style, but you might have to turn your bandmates on to the music you are interested in. If you perform live, you will probably be most comfortable playing in a band that acts and dresses naturally, with no choreographed moves or costumes. Because of your interest in all kinds of music, new and old, and your love of playing, you are sure to come up with a great sound.

GLOSSARY

backstory history or background created for a character in a story, film or band

big band large (12 to 25 members) jazz band, including brass, woodwind and rhythm instruments

blues music style featuring heavy, repetitive chords; developed by African Americans in the United States

breakbeat small instrumental sequence found in most pop, funk and R&B songs

British Invasion period during the mid-1960s when a lot of bands from the United Kingdom went to the United States and became very successful. The Beatles and The Rolling Stones were two of these bands.

call and response from an African-American slave tradition, where the leader of a group and other band members alternate performing parts of a song

Civil Rights Movement period in the 1960s when black Americans stood up and fought against unfair laws

dubstep style of music with strong bass lines and slow rhythms that came from London in the early 2000s

fan base artist's or band's core group of fans

genre style or type of music

gimmick trick or stunt used by many artists to stand out from the crowd

glam rock style of rock music from the early 1970s that featured outrageous fashion, make-up and theatrics

influential inspiring or important to someone else's work

jamming when a band spontaneously plays together to see where the sound goes

jazz style of music with strong but often irregular rhythm that is part composed and part improvised (made up while being played)

karaoke game where people sing along to popular songs in front of an audience

lyrics words of a song

melody main tune of a song

plagiarism copying another person's work without permission

producer someone who creates the backing music on recorded tracks or works with a band during the recording process

R&B rhythm and blues; a form of music that started in the 1940s and blended blues, gospel and soul music

record pressed black disc, made out of a type of plastic called vinyl, on which recorded music can be stored and replayed. Records are popular with DJs.

reggae slow-tempo, rhythmic style that originated in Jamaica

rhythm strong, regular, repeated pattern of sound

riff short, repeated melody in a song that is played on an instrument

rock and roll style of loud popular music featuring several electric guitars, that first originated in the 1950s

ska genre from Jamaica that blends jazz and R&B with more traditional Caribbean music, such as calypso

sub-genre further break down of musical styles. If country is a genre, country pop is a sub-genre.

turntable object a (vinyl) record is put on, to play it; sometimes also called a record player

FIND OUT MORE

Books

Music: The Definitive Visual History (Dorling Kindersley, 2013)

Popular Culture: 2000 and Beyond (History of Popular Culture), Nick Hunter (Raintree, 2012)

Punk: Music, Fashion, Attitude! (Culture in Action!), Charlotte Guillain (Raintree, 2011)

Websites

www.freemusicarchive.org
This website has a massive collection of free music from all genres and eras.

www.furia.com/misc/genremaps
On this website there is an interactive map of many genres and sub-genres. You can click on each one and see many of the artists playing in this genre.

www.girlrocknation.com
Girl Rock Nation is a great resource for young women who want to rock!

www.music-map.com
On this fun website you can type in the name of any artist or band and it will show the bands that influenced the artist as well as bands that were influenced by the artist.

DVD

Ziggy Stardust and the Spiders from Mars: The Motion Picture (1973)
This movie documents the last concert that David Bowie performed as Ziggy Stardust.

Place to visit

The British Music Experience
www.britishmusicexperience.com
This is a museum of popular music, located at the O2 in London.
Using cutting edge audio-visual technology, visitors can trace historic
and era-defining moments through 60 years of music history.

Index